When I Was Just A Little Girl

Krystal Marionakis
Author, Illustrator, and Photographer

PAGE PUBLISHING
Conneaut Lake, PA

First originally published by Page Publishing 2022

ISBN 978-1-6624-7932-8 (pbk)
ISBN 978-1-6624-7933-5 (digital)

Printed in the United States of America

This book is dedicated to my incredible family who has guided me through life each and every day; and my little best friend, my daughter, Lucia Grace.

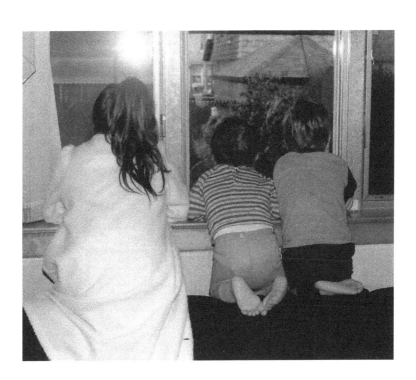

When I was just a little girl,
I learned to crawl before I walked
And gurgle before I talked.

3

When I was just a little girl,
I learned grown-up food was great!
And if I had to use the bathroom...
I would have to wait.

When I got a little older,
My daddy told me, "Ladies chew
with their mouths closed."
"My mom must be a lady!"
I supposed.

Then, I had a little brother
And my mom would say,
"Share, share, that's what's fair!"

All I could think was,
"You don't know he pulls my hair!"

My daddy told me not to
talk to strangers.
He helped me understand they
could be danger.

11

"You get more with sugar
than with vinegar!"
my mom would say.
"I don't understand that,
no how, no way!"

"Give up my lollipop?
Oh! Stop!"

13

Then my second brother came
and I understood...
If I treated him with kindness, I
would get something good!

15

My mom taught me how important
it is to dress pretty. She says,
"You never know who you may
see in this city!"

"Confidence and happiness is key!"
If I put those on first,
I'll stay pretty as can be!

"You're beautiful,"
my daddy says,
"but it's what's on the
inside that counts!"

I looked inside my mouth, and
there was no beauty there,
not even an ounce!

19

I made my brother a special gift
on his first day of school.
It was hard for him to part.

"You see!" my daddy said,
"You have a beautiful heart!"

21

At night, Mom squeezed me tight
and told me "One day we'll be
best friends, you know?
Good friends may come and go, but
I will always love you so."

23

Mommy always says, "Che sera sera..."
Whatever will be, will be...
Now, I understand, the future is
not ours to see.

My dad could always feel my fear,
so one day he whispered in my ear,

"Everything you need
is right inside of you."

I hit that ball over the fence, and
right then, I think I knew.

"You're my hero,"
my daddy says to me.
"How? I don't even have one
superpower. That can't be!"

29

I climbed into my daddy's lap
and giggled as he smiled.
Finally, I understood, I am his
hero because I am his child.

Listen to your parents, kids.
Put on the jacket; it is cold out.
Because they said so and they
love you, that's why.

About the Author

Krystal Marie Marionakis grew up in Brooklyn, New York, which is where all of the inspiration behind her photographs and illustrations are from. She has two brothers, Andrew and Michael, and two loving parents, Harry and Maria, who helped her learn these important lessons, through play or sometimes the hard way. She is married to a loving husband, Salvatore, and they have a daughter named Lucia Grace, who inspires her to be the best version of herself every day, as well as two children, through marriage, Giuliana and Giovanni, who she loves very much.

Krystal is an NYC DOE teacher and has always found it fascinating how much is learned at home that carries over into her classroom each year. She has taught English as a second language for eight years now and thrives on learning about new cultures, traditions, religions, and languages. Everyone is different, but everyone has learned from the people they love. Disclaimer: Krystal is still learning.

CPSIA information can be obtained
at www.ICGtesting.com
Printed in the USA
JSHW051924220323
39311JS00005B/58